Advanc

Sarah Patterson's poems take us on a life journey, ridding the self of shame and unanswered questions to arrive at tenderness. It is a tenderness "written by blisters," and we can thank the poet for being "a bundle so versatile" that her words—unabashed and vibrant—hold up a mirror to us all.

— Lisa Vihos, poet laureate, Sheboygan, WI

If you've ever paid attention to neighbor kids, men interrupting women, skateparks, or the sorrow of a shopping cart full of personal belongings, you will feel these poems in your bones. Sarah Patterson's collection *What Color Am I?* asks a question, but it really sees answers. These poems observe. Then they report in rich, welcome language. They see color. They see human interactions. These poems greet the reader like plumeria, then prick us with thorns. They break us with family photographs, then hold us like cast iron. Anyone who yearns to pay attention to human life will find a friend in this book.

— Joseph Ross, author of *Ache* and *Raising King*

A fascinating collection, taking the reader through an often troubled and troubling range of emotions, memories, voices, and experiences, ferociously honest and tenderly, even affectionately considerate at the same time. Powerful, unsettling poems that confront one's own misgivings, one's self-doubts, inculcated, then self-cultivated, but in the process of their recognition torn out and banished to let the human spirit free, the individual self to assert itself. Poems that don't turn their face away from what is ordinary, what is harsh, messy, and not so pretty, in families and received social norms of race, color, class, and gender, to find, to rise into, as the collection proceeds, beauty, genuine pluck and luminosity. Poignant, plain-spoken, and memorable. Sarah Patterson's "What Color Am I?" is a remarkable testimonial of triumph and affirmation.

— Waqas Khwaja, Ellen Douglass Leyburn
Professor of English, Agnes Scott College

What Color Am I? is a triumphant cocoon of poetry encapsulating issues such as, but not limited to, race, beauty ideals, divorce, and alcoholism. Patterson has constructed a thought-provoking, modern day feminist collection of literary excellence.

— Lauren Eileen, author of *Lauren and Val Take
a Walk*

As I read *What Color Am I?*, I was transported to New Mexico and offered a heart-wrenching account of the author's life. Alcoholism, racism, sexism and family dynamics are brought to bear in this important poetry collection. These are poems I will read again and again, learning something new and important each time.

— Jill Celeste, MA, author of *Loud Woman: Goodbye, Inner Good Girl!*

What Color Am I? is a bold debut poetry collection that explores the themes of identity, gender, and capitalism, all undergirded by a constant connection to the deserts of the west. Sarah Patterson's poems offer a raw and honest exploration of the complexities of racial identity, problematizing what the modern United States loves to simplify as black and white. What does it mean to be in a female body? What has capitalism done to our humanity? And what of the land—of your ancestors, of your birth, of your growth?

— Constanza Ontaneda

What Color Am I?

What Color Am I?

Sarah Patterson, M.F.A.

Foreword by
Dr. Tyson Hausdoerffer

HIGHLANDER
PRESS

ISBN: 978-1-956442-07-6
Ebook ISBN: 978-1-956442-08-3
Library of Congress Control Number: 2022938733

Published by Highlander Press
501 W. University Pkwy, Ste. B2
Baltimore, MD 21210

Cover design: Patricia Creedon
Cover collage: Mel Nakamura (@fallenstar.photography)

To my grandmother Elizabeth, for showing me warmest blood in my veins and saying, "This is our family, this is our heritage, this is where you begin."

Contents

III.

Foreword

Dr. Tyson Hausdoerffer

In this audacious debut collection, author Sarah Patterson takes the reader on a lively and often unsettling journey through the conflicted landscape of contemporary America. While it is a collection rather than a continuous narrative, the experience it offers when read cover to cover is, for this reader at least, akin to the experience of reading a gritty, searching American road novel such as Jack Kerouac's *On the Road*, or, to trace the road novel's lineage further back, it's reminiscent in some ways of early modern narratives like the anonymous *Lazarillo de Tormes* or Daniel Defoe's *Moll Flanders*. In other words, this collection has more than a touch of the picaresque to it.

I mention this because it was not until I recognized that I was listening to the voice of a contemporary American *pícara*, that I felt the full power and understood the real significance of Sarah's work. Like the *pícaros* of the great picaresque works of the past, the "I" that speaks to us throughout *What Color Am I?* comes from an underprivileged and somewhat enigmatic background (the sepia photo in the poem "even the cast iron knows" is emblematic of this), suffers the disintegration of her family (see especially "garage"), and is thrust into an unwelcoming and sometimes hostile world where she must fend for herself (see for example "two-fold shame"). Like traditional *pícaros*, she travels widely (from New Mexico and Colorado to Hawaii and beyond), and she uses her wits—and her *wit*—to make her way through various levels of society, from mobile homes and skateparks to "middle class IKEA twilight zone[s]" and even a yacht club. Like them, she survives numerous encounters with unsavory figures and endures repeated attempts by society at large to define her, to categorize her, to *color* her (see for example "recipe for a mixed race girl" or "gym motivation"). Yet, like the natural curl in her hair that refuses to be tamed (as we hear in "trim"), she always bounces back in defiance.

But to describe the "I" of this collection as *only* a contemporary American *pícara* is to participate in the very efforts to define, categorize, confine, and pin down that she so persistently resists. In any case, the attentive reader will immediately sense that she exceeds the static and limited character of traditional *pícaros*. Although she possesses their sharp wit, sardonic humor, and incisive ability to see things for what they really are (the poems "man interrupting" and "title ix" come immediately to mind), she never lapses into self-centeredness, as so many *pícaros* do. No, in poems such as "desert showers," where she "learns lessons from the weeds," and "garage," where she is able to see the significance of the crayons amid the "smell of regret / potent in cluttered corners," we see that she never loses her openness to the world around her, nor her ability to empathize with others.

Even more importantly, though, and very unlike any *pícaro*, she never allows her encounters with the sordid and corrupt dimensions of society to make her cynical or to destroy her desire for a better, more just world. Her righteous indignation at the casual misogyny and racism she encounters wherever she goes comes through powerfully in poems like "lip service" and "names men call me," to name just two. In poems such as "women in space" (possibly the collection's centerpiece), that righteous indignation gives rise to full-fledged, hard-hitting satire of the Juvenalian variety, while in poems such as "even the cast iron knows," righteous indignation gives way to sympathetic inquiry and ends with the plaintive statement that "nobody knows my name." In other words, this collection displays all the satirical insight of a good picaresque novel but none of its typical and depressing cynicism.

Like any strong collection of poetry, *What Color Am I?* can be read in many ways, and, in this brief foreword, I have tried to share with you, the reader, just one way in which it might be approached and enjoyed: as a mosaic-like narrative that foregrounds a "picaresque-plus" persona. But however you end up approaching it, I have no doubt that you will find a great variety of pleasure in the experience. You will at times be moved to sorrow and at times be brought to laughter, but you will always be challenged by the voice in these poems to feel and think differently about your own journey through the American experience.

And that is the greatest gift a collection can offer its readers—the gift of feeling and thinking differently. Reader, enjoy!

Tyson Hausdoerffer , Ph.D.
Director of the Graduate Program in Creative Writing at Western Colorado University and a translator of Ancient Greek poetry

I.

recipe for a mixed race girl

3 Tbsp European*
1 drop of Black**
1 pinch Native American
6 cups White***

whisk until well combined
a consistent batter of confusion,
people won't know what to call her
skin should be caramel in color
be careful not to burn, she'll be too dark
don't let the white overwhelm the features
but let it have control of the voice
the black will be a nice surprise
the hint of native refreshing

cook her on the back burner
leave there until cooled
some say fire her longer
some will say she's not dark enough
call her a White Passing, a tasteful excuse
or if you're kind, call her a Creole

drizzle a little extra black blood
sprinkle a little more Choctaw
for a first glance's sake
best served in solitude

*use only if defensive
**substitute any other colored ingredients
***don't forget the white

trim

I tell the hair stylist
my hair is curly
but she sees frizz
she sees a wave
something like a curl
but too straight
too recently flat-ironed
too fearful of its nature
so she reaches for those edgers
the ones with teeth
made to separate
to cast aside
to lift away the weight
of texture, of curl
of my hair's desire to bend
to twist off my scalp
even when I scorch her
bleach her, hot white

tell her she's too unpredictable
she curls around me
protects me
I cut her off anyway

even the cast iron knows

smooth nameless photographs
layers of sepia on dusted faces

I never find out
what color I am

what color am I?
my question glides

my grandmother's eyes
are closed and in the river

Metoyers soak in Cane River
only they know their names

only Natchitoches knows Metoyer
and its sounds of escape

like farm gates opening
like money in pockets

Metoyers know churches
know mansions with freedom

a privilege of white passing
Metoyers know best

their history unwrinkles
from my grandmother's mouth

Metoyers know plantations
and call them farms,

but what color are they?
I ask my grandmother

what color are you?
she responds, anything but black

cast iron sweats on the stove
even it knows its burn is black

she shows me sepia photographs
erasure in white palms

with willow root knuckles bent
around memories folded out

layers of brown in the sun
burned by the truth of light

creoles hide in tones
free to their dreams

the name Patterson
tucked in a white blanket

a black photo with a white name
I am not black like my grandfather

was not black
under the name Patterson

could not be a Carry because
it burned his willow roots and

lightskins still need jobs
need *white passing* to work

black faces still see the sun
under the brim of a hat

Metoyers and Pattersons
don't show up in photographs

because they are not brown
like the sepia is not brown

it does not show black colors
that photographs darken in a flash

somehow the sun burns
somehow the sun fades

somehow I do not know
what color am I?

I do not show up in sepia
I do not flash in the sun

there are no burns on my body
and nobody knows my name

movie star teeth

I have nine cavities
I can't eat sweets
or drink cold water
flossing makes me bleed

bad teeth are genetic
braces, spacers, root canals
nail biting and alcoholism
family faults now mine

holes bored in teeth
erode smiles and enamel
more pain of mouth
my cavities multiplied early

I wore a spacer
when I was seven
had braces put in
when I was sixteen

finally, my teeth straight
adult molars grown in
finally, my father said
you can be someone

we can make you
a pretty movie star
file your teeth
straight, flat, perfect

I could be perfect
think of the possibilities
flat teeth can offer me
and so I dreamt

of all the nothingness
flat teeth can bring
I thought of drills
and files on bone

background whirs
of a dental montage
my mind a flashback
chewed up in back molars

my father's bad breath
erupted in my nose
as we napped together
on our 90s futon

the only house furniture
he kept for himself
divorce rotted him away
alcohol, always an ablution

I have always wondered
where my teeth go
when they fall out
in my realest dreams

all my mother's teeth
impeccable, straight, white
but before her perfection
she championed fangs

no money for braces
until it came from
pockets filled with shame
a necessity for vanity

I'm woken by sounds
of a woman scraping
pressing prodding my gums
wounds of negligence galore

all of my cavities
have throbbed for years
yet I subdued them
with sensodyne toothpaste

floss crafted like handcuffs
and I blame them
for stealing my pleasures
snickers bars, gummy bears

what good are teeth
when they are flat?
how can you fight
with filed down fangs

movie stars with no plaque
no memories like cavities
they do not dream
of losing their teeth

to dream of
disappearing teeth
is to dream
of losing your voice

this is a loss
some mouths never suffer
my parents do not
dream of teeth either

my father dreams only
himself in a bottle
trapped by the memories
he gargles and spits

my mother dreams only
of a different life
where all her mistakes
vanish down her throat

whether it be by
bottle or by throat
I vanish between bites
in my parents' mouths

but who's to say
I am a mistake
maybe I'm just black
a cavity there

hidden in their molar
something to fill in
with wisdoms of cement
and false color

my father doesn't want
a movie star daughter
just one with teeth
flat enough to convince

maybe I wanted them
pristine celebrity dreams
maybe I am responsible
for shadows in my smile

but, a cavity is still
a negative space
a gap inside me
that wasn't there before

desert showers

the clouds witnessed me
try to fill the arroyos,
they sent me pity

and creosote bush
nature's peaceful reminder
of those happy tears

rain when the sun's out
a young girl in the desert
learns lessons from weeds

electricat

I had a vicious dog when I was young
his name was Stinger and he would run off
Into the desert on his four dry paws
only to return when the sun was gone
down behind the organ mountains beside
my house Stinger would abide by no one
my father had picked him up from the road
when he was young, still he never listened
My mother refused to chain him outside
in the dry heat of our Las Cruces home
she let him roam the yard when he was alone
Away he would run that golden mutt dog
to kill the neighbors' chickens in their yards
to dismember the day like any dog
with owners who could care less about him
and children who did not know how to care
A wild creature with wrinkles on his head
his tongue was spotted purple like a chow
his ears were oddly small and folded down

I sometimes saw that little ray of light
He waited for us at the door or fence
and we fed him most days, to our defense
he hadn't the need, but ate from our hands
he licked our fingers and jumped to our chest
he was our Stinger, just like any dog

One Sunday evening there came a cat
he was walking on our telephone wire
A circus act for desert life below
the cat blended with the sun as it fell
just another piece of the sun setting
another shed of light tracing the sky
Our golden dog did not seem thrilled by him
such an audacious cat he must have thought
to not only sneak into his home base
but to do so with such ginger prowess
That Stinger was so stung he howled up
as the cat took his perch above the yard
to our dog's surprise the cat meowed back
and did not stop until late that dark night
That same night there was a heavy rainstorm
thunder seemed to reach for our feline friend
yet stinger did not come into the porch
we never let him inside anyway
this one night I begged my mother just so,
Please can we let the dog in mom, there's rain
she simply shook her head and said to me
No, we can't he'd be an absolute pain
I looked through every window in my house
before skulking off to my bedroom last

I stayed awake with the storm that cold night
sometimes catching faint meows in my ears

I knew that dog must be below the pole
awaiting the company of the cat
Once my mind drifted off it happened
a snap that nothing in the desert makes
This followed by the victim's tortured screech
I ran into my mother's bedroom fast
and found my brother also hidden there
It was not till morning that we would find
that bold ginger cat hung with the sunrise
His foot was caught by the telephone wire
melded there by lightning's hands of hot fire
frozen in an infinite leap outward
his small paws reaching to a spot not found
almost worse there too was our dog Stinger
He had lost all his barks to the night rain
and now sat still eyes focused on the cat
He was waiting for his prey to reach him
down in the dust and weeds of our backyard

So what was done of the poor ginger cat?
he was left there all Monday, petrified
The electric company came at five
to remove that sad beast that dangled there
and we thought that this ordeal would end there
this was not the case, the company came
it was sunset again as they rose up
The men met minimum expectations
once they'd wrangled that cat from its wire
They did not bring him down in their basket
They did not cradle his stiff lifeless bod
the electricians just released his leg
to this day I wonder if cats have souls
I pray that his ginger soul left his heart
The cat fell down into the yard below

and by now you should know who was waiting
My dog Stinger bided his time that dusk
he let the electricians leave in peace
once they were gone he took hold of that corpse
My mom took us inside to spare our eyes
as the dog tore across the yard with it
I remember its stiff body flying
He flew back and forth in our yard until
he did become weary of its lifeless corpse
then he retired under our porch content
to spend the last hours slow and dreaming
soft sunlight left him there to rise again
tomorrow when he'd come and greet the day

roadkill

I saw a dead horse with his legs above
his body, crooked from all directions.
It was so sad to see those large horseshoes
dangle. Dogs I've seen and cats I see most.
The horse was such a surprise to me while
I drove the dry path to Alamosa.
It was so disturbing, being dead out there.
I had to stop and contemplate his corpse.
Its legs were rigid, much too rigid for
a horse of lovely stature. Very strange
I pondered, who has left you here to die?
Then something weird occurred, a voice I heard.
It came from beneath my eyes to my shock
the horse had responded to my query
"I was not left here silly human girl,
I fell." This caught me off guard quite a bit
I leapt back from his speaking body fast.
The horse laughed loudly, "Well you did ask me."

neighbor kids

mama let the neighbors over once
we felt rich an afternoon
they spent hours on our gamecube
she even made monkey bread
our mouths glazed over with laughter
so what if I only got one cinnamon pearl
for a moment we were plucked
from the nowhere of butterfly lane
when a nail found itself
under my brother's foot
in their backyard and
I bent my nose on their trampoline
my mother started to wonder
what else they could break
her children's toys
locks on her cabinets
our mistakes shut the door on
midday snacks lingering play dates
their mobile home became spectacle

the house of horrors
their poverty a spectacle
filled with empty mirrors and
the sound of change escaping jars
mama told us
they can't come in
their hands were *made of dirt*
only invited
through broken windows
mama told me
lock our doors
to keep the dirt out
but, I found another way
to let the desert in

coyote sonnet

my loss of you is like my loss of home
which is to say not at all. why do you
believe me ignoble when you are too
a thief of devotion, an antinome

and when amity lost its trinity
your prickly fingers held true to the yoke.
me, left for coyotes and my lead broke.
what sweet alabaster skull laxity

now your twin dust swims through my eye socket
searching for an attentive or fond gaze
you tug my horns gently along with strain
with eyes so easy to interpret
I swallowed them, with no grass to graze
why look for eyes here when you hold my gain

garage

we're cleaning it out
three brooms gliding around
nudie mags, smirnoff shooters
scraps of my father's shame
a pile has formed, my brother and I
are wind chime echoes
hung by his old desk shelves
the color of old liberty
my mother is a rising heat
this is release, in sweat, in voice
breasts in slick magazine pages
explain how divorce ends with disgust

she wants me to see
playboy bunnies and cigarette boxes
tools dusted with the quiet sadness
of two souls parting ways
and the smell of regret
potent in cluttered corners

a shadow of adult behavior
but I only see crayons
a graveyard of crayola on his desk
reflections on the wall by name
scarlet
clementine
indigo
pink

my father's thoughts
reduced to wax
addictions melted to hours,
years of his thoughts
scribbled to a wall
years of my memories
lost in this garage, a face
remains the most familiar
what's to know besides addiction,
a golden Sunday morning or two,
rides home in the bed of his Chevy
license plate RUNVS2
who wouldn't be

this intentional vilification
of a man who collected rattlesnake tales
and stole time traveling street signs
who kept an upright horseshoe
and prayed it'd be enough
my mother took it down
thrust his belongings into darkness
and found my father was already waiting there
a round lamplight oozing from those walls

I was never allowed in the garage
never allowed to see my father
in the light

II.

eye rolls

your eyes spin like a buffer screen, all backward
like so over bleak vibrations of being
like so totally over this existence
nineteen years of iPhones and suffering
giggle turned groan at thoughts of trying
to be anything but miserable
all you wanted was spaghetti straps and
some money for your body, just hold your tongue
save your voice for yourself, and laugh later
at jokes that serve you, that catch you
whites of your eyeballs, a camera click, no picture
just the glare of blank screens, the flash
not enough likes, shares or retweets
why would you care?, you're busy
scrolling through lists of people you dread
your parents, your boyfriend, your teacher
your innocence instantly instagrammable
tack it on your face, save their feelings

let eye veins grasp for irises and plead return
when your pupils descend from the cloud, think
who am I really here for?

women in space

to us life is zero gravity
boots magnetized to floors
we float between doorways

hover over seats
in space   men don't want us
thought we'd run out of oxygen
get sucked back in to nothing

     maybe
men hoped we'd become air
so they didn't have to share
or waste an eternity
of breathing on women

they must think
if women are allowed on earth
why do they need more   space?

on buses, airplanes, subways
sidewalks to stretch their limbs out

we bubble our heads in space
suck up our limbs hold our breath
it's harder to hear us that way
harder to say *excuse me, sir*

and when legroom gets scarce
men seem to get closer
maybe that's why they love space
expanding the width from knee   to   knee

there's no room for women in space
when earth has to store our bodies
to make room for more men
they put us in the ground

so our limbs won't grow onto
airplane armrests and park benches
how dare we need more   space
more air to suffocate with
all we asked for was to breathe
with lungs and mouths of our own
it's no wonder in space
we can't scream

two-fold shame

the discomfort I feel
when a man reveals his wallet
unfolds my anxiety
tucks it in my underwear

I pretend not to sell myself
folded into a table

I watch a man pay for me
put the money in my hands
there's something about fingers
diving into green crevices

filth left under fingernails
ends up in the eyes

I am not needy
he didn't say that

but wallets seem to whisper
they gasp about me

go on and spend his money
it's what he wants to do

credit cards are guiltless
the more benjamins the better
I'm shaking him down
holding him up at the counter

all I have to do for food
is lend my skin for an hour

he'll pay for my dinner
my alcohol, my latte
what do I deserve?
if not allowed my body

if he pays you have to
shake his hand, make a deal
a woman's responsibility
a curse like dessert
sweet, unnecessary
another leather notch

my time isn't enough?
he has to take my body too

but, his goal isn't insult
no micro-aggression
compliments become weakness
vulnerability a requirement

with a fake laugh worth $50.00
and index finger down the arm

eyes away when checks come
a girl who knows
a plastic lifestyle
where men turn out their pockets

denim scratches leather
who crinkles, me or the dollars?

man interrupting

It was just a joke!
every time someone says
that word *rape*
a man gets arrested

every time somebody
touches some body
a court date is scheduled
a man is on the line

always ladies telling me *no*
hardly even a word
n o
hardly even two letters

N O
barely in your mouth
on your tongue
barely a breath

I'd rather be inside your mouth
use your tongue like that
forget that word
I didn't put it there

flick your tongue
let go of it no
you women should really talk
about men being assaulted

where's our #HeToo movement
where's our tongues
where's our freedom in jaws
of women, of liars, of most

not all men do that
not all men make rape jokes
unless it'll get laughs
with the boys

not all women suck
you blow me away
with that useless *no*
some women love me

they crinkle down in
giggles in cocktail dresses
my dates get the joke
with open mouths they let me in

a vocal vice grip
are you still talking?

gym motivation

why lift weights when i can't lift my head
somedays i hate society and sundays
i drag my knuckles around 45 lb bars
and hope the tendons in my knees don't shred

why risk failure
knee failure heart failure, all bodily
to fit into a size small crop top. around me
forever 21 mannequins check the mirror

i could lift my 168 lbs elsewhere
away from men's reflections four feet behind me
their stares aren't worth barbell grime
more reminders of why i'm even here

society is just another 45 lb plate
waiting for me to put on my spandex and pretend
i don't see my muffin top as i bend
men in society just want a chance at my weight

why sweat when life drips down my nose
and my ass, what's another pr
another 10 lbs added onto the bar
when every woman knows

life would fuck me at a size 10 or size 4
life doesn't care if my thighs align
life can't count pounds calories or dollar signs
life can't read the weight on the bar

why lift weights when society breaks the scales
when i stand naked in my bathroom i still sweat
because life can lift me at fluctuating weight
life hits the gym more than it hits the showers

why lift weights when life reeks
when life is the sweatiest dude in the gym size XXL
when life only wants my ass to be XXL
what's another 100 lunges until my knee squeaks

why lift weights when life's heavy
torn ligaments sore muscles my fracture
i posture and pose, just another capture
my form is bad and my soul is sweaty

lip service

Hear me, man at the party, watch the words fall out of my mouth, if
you have to, count the number of times I blink, I don't care what you
do, I'm talking, not to you, but you, sir, happen to be here, taking up
our space, listen to me, sir, I value ears within my vicinity so long as
mouths are not involved, this is what happens when people congre-
gate and share words not spaces in sentences, not breaths in pauses, I
will not share my commas with you sir, my *likes* and *ums* are not
places worthy of your offenses, your *what I thinks* or your *actuallys*
they are me, gathering my thoughts, I can assure you my voice is
louder, I will not condescend to you sir, I will walk away while you
are speaking, leave your opinions to silence, your interruptions aren't
worth the cochlea in my ears, sir, I will continue to ignore you until
my period is placed, I will make my point as you make it yours to shut
that nagging orifice you call your mouth, make it clear what you value
is nothing that you can't control, do not interrupt me sir you've had a
millennia to speak, you've had an entire history to babble and roll
over us women, who you've brandished with "chatty" with "gossipy"
with "gibbery" with "wordy" with "gabby" all of our screaming adjec-
tives that end in y, because it's the question you're begging us to ask,

why, so you can tell us something we've already heard, *why*, so we can be silent and listen to you mansplain, *why*, so we can be trapped in this conversational concentric circle for an eternity as you live out your aspiration of being captivating for another few centuries, no sir, I will ask instead, why do you believe you belong in our conversations, why do you interject yourself into our presence, why sir, do you find it so easy to force yourself into a woman's mouth, look through her eyes, speak through her lips and yet sir, how can you still not respect us, will you not allow us silence, stay in your own head sir, tear open your ears and chain your teeth together, sir, and listen to me speak.

Title IX

Adams State has a Title IX program
for sexual assault victims
to pour their tears into a pitcher and drink
they saved some students
from cat calling construction workers
they're still not finished with it
the crosswalk *where did they go?*
for the girls to walk to class
their argyle patterned tasers,
pepto-bismo pink pepper spray
kitten shaped keychain knuckles
fanged ridges choking their fingers
weapons aren't allowed on campus
guess we better learn to whistle
or pay up, maybe the lilac?
it matches her backpack

who will listen?
the police officers downstairs

are out to lunch, out to cite
just the deer and the squirrels
who are they gonna tell?
is it even worth telling the woman
yes, she is a woman
on the other side of the desk
with the empty pitcher
a crystal film around the bottom
from the last girl who swallowed
her secrets dissolved to salt
while the woman yawned
her mouth said
I won't tell anyone
her eyes said
I promise

names men call me

miss if they're a stranger
ma'am if they're younger
mrs. patterson for the students
young lady for the prudes and
sometimes I'm *that bitch over there*
other times I've been *the one with no hair*
if they're feeling bold I'm a cunt
sweetheart if they're on the hunt
I've been beautiful once before
a few times I've even been, whore
the weirdest of men called me caramel
cavewoman once because of my smell
once sarai, he was trying to impress me
once princess, he was trying to undress me
my least favorite was *jungle girl*
she-man made me want to hurl
can't forget baby, darling or sweetie
those men seemed especially needy
I'm surprised I even remember my name

but it's myself that's to blame
for being a bundle so versatile
that men can't think of one name, but still
my name's been around for many an era
it's not that fucking hard to call me Sarah

buzzed

a man dips into a bee's grocery store
he has no business there
he inhales, hands to outer petals
as if without him they would wilt
lips gently graze curling folds
a canna's best blush
on cheeks of a waiting lover

anticipation, a quiver
she opens reluctantly
his smile spreads her petals
face buried in the anther
he inhales, he pinches
plucks away her spirit
eyes folded mid bloom

does he know what he missed?
he exhales, petals close
a skirt dripped over wide hips

he releases her still chosen
trimmers fumble out of denim
thumb and index fingers to thorns
a sharp cleft, she's his

she'll wither in his palms
fall apart under his nose
collapse into a vase and wait
she weeps when he walks by
his glass holding her together
eventually he'll throw her away
unable to breathe her in, he'll exhale

braud's shoulders

atlas could never have this bod
Doña Ana horizon broad
I threw them into guts and hurled
myself into bodies, unfurled
these shoulders are not scared to goad
they'll knock you down but raise you high
they'd carry you and your burdens
all expectations they defy
and fill men with jealous omens

petal head

I.

I can caress my beloved
if I think of his eyelashes
and only let him go down
when his face is shaved

only if I imagine
breasts swelled into mountains
under his nipples, free of restriction
that roll as he moans, up and down

lips soft like a woman's
if I don't hold his jaw, I can pretend
they're covered in gloss
unstick myself from the present

drift back in sheets to new mexico
where the thunder waited for me

to know why she whispers in the sky
to know how rumbles begin

a girl's navel in the lamp light
slick windows capture musk
the bed not stained with it
that stench of man

I drift back still to heat and
red hair curtained my cheeks
hiding me from *heterosexual*
the cushion of a girl's mouth

calluses wrench my face back
sweat and smells only men emit
passion to make Aries faint
shame comes with completion

it dawns his presence
my pleasure leaks away
as I drip into his hands
he suspects nothing

II.

those flowers in my brain
bulbless emotions with stems
I'd have to yank them up
find where the roots clench

he knows nothing of hydrangeas
dressed in navy sweaters

petals warm with lazuli
bushels bound to the edges

he knows only of my irises
flowers I willingly give
he knows, I am eternally purple
the wrinkles split from my legs

my beloved wishes for more
roses, to make room for sweet days
for his thorns in my planters
such simple pathetic things

I planted them away from me
my irises will not choke
at the roots of needy bushels
predictable, unwilling to grow

my beloved only sees irises
with wilted frills and skewer leaves
he sees that I am happy with him
toil of consistent pricks

roses with expectations
and a need for explanation
roses with all their familiarity
bloom through my eyes

petals from every man I've loved
wrinkled below to feed him
my garden a graveyard of freedom
a cemetery of those stupid roses

I like to have sex with my beloved
when his eyelashes are petals
and his roses bloom
without thorning my irises

protection

I like what you're doing with that bandana
she held her arm up and pointed

I felt guilt for internally scoffing
when she mentioned it was also protection

nobody needs protection at a yacht club
maybe from drowning, easy, don't breathe

but she continued, mentioned that she knew
why I wore it, why I picked the color red

why it wasn't so much about Rosie
and more about being seen

her name was Elizabeth, she told me
about how witches wore bandanas

about covering your head from evil energy
about minding your surroundings for signs

Elizabeth told me my name was biblical
and when I told her I hated that she laughed, or tried

when I told her I was called Sarai once she froze
being the inventor of the patriarchy is raw

in her eyes I could see the clouds of her memories
drifting away with the water past the pier

she told me the club members kept telling her stories
about how she was named after a saint

or maybe just a martyr, they can't all be winners
told me she was named after someone who

hung herself. a man had told her,
this man tells all the waitresses where they come from

Elizabeth looked at my bandana when she said it
then said *hung herself* again, and I blinked by mistake

when she said she'd been thinking about it
when she picked up the butter knife I dropped

and held it in her hands, just held it
I wondered if what she meant was true

that my bandana would protect me from bad energy
if it would protect me from imagining Elizabeth

her neck in one of the boaters ropes gasping
It was weird, like he knew I had been planning it

every time Elizabeth eyed me I felt my bandana
slipping from my head to my neck

when they fired her two days later I checked my throat
put away my bandanas and prayed for protection

in came the rain

alright, you win
I cannot escape your
fisheye drops magnifying me,
a depiction of sadness
leaking through the walls

I can hear you,
coming to drown me
still straight dripping
meek water dancing
with gravity, feeding me

I'm rushing to fill glass cups
with you, I'll save my tears
for a happier day or hour
after you've drifted off
to ruin another car wash

become another excuse
to stay inside, to watch
my reflection feed the earth
a chaotic downpour

III.

plumeria

it would be wrong
to compare a plumeria
to a haole, white
sometimes sunburnt
blushed around the neck
face down on asphalt
focused on what they've done
fallen from origins
planted long before they arrived

every week they appear
fresh, blank and unaware
and every week they're scraped up
and replaced with more
scattered about the island
being picked up by locals
placed behind their ears
taxied with the greatest care

sometimes added to leis
proudly worn on chests
or hakus, begging to be noticed
to be admired, to be symbols
of a culture they never knew
of an island they didn't come from
to be rested on the lawns
and lands of bare indigenous feet
nurtured by aloha
passed between native fingers

not a pandemic poem

I will not write a pandemic poem
there is too much time to think about it

too much time to think about that virus
the president won't even wear a mask

one mask too many for the president
poetic resources would be wasted

my poems deserve more resources and
acceptance hidden behind a man's mask

only some are safe under all these masks
I will not hear it, unprecedented

unprecedented, a horrible lie
one more mask for my pandemic poem

I will not write that goddamn poem
there is too much time to waste on it

shopping cart

litter never looked so useful
abandoned on a curb

so many holes
who could fill it?

who wants everyone to see
what they carry?

or what they leave behind
unfulfilled baskets

dreams rolling through streets
catch a passerby glance

accustomed to emptiness
it rolls by

moniker of homelessness
pack mule of possessions

and imaginary burdens
wheeled vessel motionless

no ultimatums here
just empty or not

here it comes your reminder
how little you could have

in moment long decisions
how much you could give

if you slowed your roll
and emptied your cart

IKEA nightmare

rooms no one has lived in
and never will
fever dream for housewives
aspiring young women
what's worse is the full drawers
full with too much already
furnished for a lifetime
there could be hundreds
housed on couches alone
hundreds more in beds
IKEA can sell false junk drawers
they could sell the air
the only thing Ikea doesn't sell
is sag and scuff
butt imprints of entitlement
smells of skin
wrinkles in comfort
pushes itself into wood
into fabric, such costly surfaces

in middle class IKEA twilight zone
fluorescent lights flash
imitating the sunrise
the sun flickers on
more things bought
for already filled homes
why waste space...furniture
rooms full of futons
for nobody to sleep on
pristine kitchenettes
no-one wants to afford
do somebody a favor, IKEA
let the homeless in
beds should be slept in
hundreds of homes in one
what's one store overrun
filled with people who actually need
what's one charity space
then the furniture will be real
will have the wear and tear
of a home worth belonging to

slow lights

pluck me from concrete
I am curb filth
like dandelions
I'm a nuisance

but they love me
I'm everywhere
sufferer on street corner
being yellow for anyone

who cares to notice slow lights
flower crown for grass puller
ear adornment for traveler
lying there petals splayed

being yellow for anyone
sufferer on street corner
I'm everywhere
but they love me

I'm a nuisance
like dandelions
I am curb filth
pluck me from concrete

skatepark thoughts

I don't care if I break
my ankle, my arm, my leg

this happens every time
wheel on the coping

I don't mind the damage
so what if I eat it

concrete can't scare me with
broken promises of pain

assured injuries or falls
a break wouldn't be so bad

a break means I can't walk, maybe
can't function all day

just a break, a fracture
hairline in my schedule, a crack

a pause in momentum
a rock in front of my wheel

I don't fear my broken body
I don't fear a taste of the end

it's just time after all,
a break from my reality

sunday afternoon

I re-wear my black sex pistols t-shirt
until it's exhausted
little gray girls in hammocks
under my eyes
the collar got the worst of
my current bed-mate's sweat stains
left shoulder looks like a raisin
smells like onions

blue floral undies turned
abstract feminist art
home to irresponsible blood stains
spread herself wide in the cotton
and bore her soul
only to be sneered at
by the person who left her there

toiletries attacked the denim
when I wasn't looking

between New Mexico and Colorado
they drowned my youngest shorts
lavender turned chloroform
limp bodied the waistline sags

all pairs of socks
now belong in the trash
filthy crumpled balls of thread
crush in the stories
written by blisters
overgrown toenails
flaking heel skins
stench tried to overwrite them
and nearly succeeded

pond scum

my eyes bounce off your bottom lip
gaze pops into green ponds
frogs plink
dip in the water
who lives there
those murky olive glances
civilization under your lily lids
searching the green
amidst cattails and ripples
coys laugh at me
for staring too long
under circle after chipped circle
my head breast strokes through
pink lips like lotuses
spin closed at night fall

shark's cove

don't touch anything
pretend you're in a museum
you know not to touch
most man made creations
God must not exist
when man is on vacation

we'll drift past exhibits
here in the cove
they'll drift past you
if you misbehave
the urchins will charge you
in venom and sting

the only sharks that swim here
have removable fins
don't forget the eels
and the waves above

ready to crack your spine
over coral cemeteries, rocks

this is how nature should be
difficult to access
safe from human hands
we had trees, birds, flowers
not enough, we want water
we want to guzzle the ocean

let go of that here
keep your hands off the earth
admire pinks, yellows, teals
accept your footless place
and leave before the cove
changes its mind

sound off

I.

I couldn't stand the finches'
constant chirp and chatter
so loud for an island
it wasn't supposed to be like this
riddled with traffic cones
and neon yellow shirts, a disease
I was nauseated with sound
too much concrete built into sand
it's a wonder the palm trees still sway
lawn mower vibrations interrupt the breeze

II.

I think of New Mexico often
gravel yards and the flagstone

between my mother's planters
adobe houses and teal door frames
their stability, I begged for arroyos
and their gaping silence
and the empty echo of home
as I swallow thousands of new faces
and beg for the sound of quail
sprinting across a desert trail

Acknowledgments

Without the help of my community, I could never imagine that I'd not only be completing this book but publishing it. Thanks to the support from my family and their many influences in my life, I was able to draw out the experiences and moments spoken in these poems. Mainly, I would like to send a thank you to my grandmother Elizabeth, who has now passed on, but will be forever immortalized in my work and in my heart. She truly brought me the gifts of roots and memories of my Creole family; this book would be a shred of light in the dark without her.

I would also like to offer a thank you to my academic community and the many eyes and ears who supported my book from its early stages as a thesis. Beginning from Aaron Abeyta, who sparked and inspired much of my stylistic choices, to Tyson Hausdoerffer, who helped me sharpen and refine my skills as a poet. I am grateful and indebted to them. I would also like to acknowledge Deborah Kevin who claimed me from the start and gave me the confidence to take my thesis to the next level.

While this list could go on forever, I would like to lastly thank those who provided offerings to my book. The many who read and gave back little pieces to this personal puzzle, without your words and your criticisms I would not have a foundation for others to understand my work. Thank you for your kindnesses and your time that you offered to be the first few involved with completing this small dream of mine.

About the Author

Sarah Patterson, M.F.A., is an emerging poet. *What Color Am I?* was written as part of Sarah's thesis as presented to the Faculty of Graduate Studies, Western Colorado University, in partial fulfillment of the requirements for the degree of Master of Fine Arts in Creative Writing. This is Sarah's first book.

 instagram.com/see.patts

About the Publisher

Highlander Press, founded in 2019, is a mid-sized publishing company committed to diversity and sharing big ideas thereby changing the world through words.

Highlander Press guides authors from where they are in the writing-editing-publishing process to where they have an impactful book of which they are proud, making a long-time dream come true. Having authored a book improves your confidence, helps create clarity, and ensures that you claim your expertise.

What makes Highlander Press unique is that their business model focuses on building strong collaborative relationships with other women-owned businesses, which specialize in some aspect of the publishing industry, such as graphic design, book marketing, book launching, copyrights, and publicity. The mantra "a rising tide lifts all boats" is one they embrace.

facebook.com/highlanderpress

instagram.com/highlanderpress

linkedin.com/in/highlanderpress

Printed in the USA
CPSIA information can be obtained
at www.ICGtesting.com
JSHW011737140124
55350JS00013B/208